CAREER DEVELOPMENT

D0523671

IMI *information service*
·dvford, Dublir ·(

T v)5̩1 ̍

Tricia Jackson BA, MSc (Personnel Management), MInstAM, FIPD is a freelance training and personnel consultant. Tricia has many years' experience as a generalist practitioner in both the public and private sectors. She is currently involved in identifying and providing training solutions, personnel consultancy, tutoring on open learning- and college-based IPD programmes, competence assessment and representing clients at employment tribunals. She is co-author of the IPD's recommended textbook for the Certificate in Personnel Practice (*Personnel Practice*, Martin and Jackson, IPD, 2nd edn, 2000) and author of two other titles in the Good Practice series: *Drugs and Alcohol Policies* (1999) and *Smoking Policies* (1999). Tricia lives in Weybridge, Surrey.

IRISH MANAGEMENT INSTITUTE LIBRARY

The Institute of Personnel and Development is the leading publisher of books and reports for personnel and training professionals, students, and all those concerned with the effective management and development of people at work. For details of all our titles, please contact the Publishing Department:

tel 020-8263 3387
fax 020-8263 3850
e-mail publish@ipd.co.uk

The catalogue of all IPD titles can be viewed on the IPD website:
http://www.ipd.co.uk/publications

CAREER DEVELOPMENT

TRICIA JACKSON

INSTITUTE OF PERSONNEL AND DEVELOPMENT

© Tricia Jackson 2000

First published in 2000

All rights reserved. No part of this publication may be reproduced,
stored in an information storage and retrieval system, or
transmitted in any form or by any means, electronic, mechanical,
photocopying, recording or otherwise, without the written
permission of the Institute of Personnel and Development, IPD
House, Camp Road, Wimbledon, London SW19 4UX.

Design and typesetting by
Wyvern 21, Bristol

Printed in Great Britain by
the Short Run Press, Exeter

British Library Cataloguing-in-Publication Data
A catalogue record for this book is available
from the British Library

ISBN 0-85292-851-3

The views expressed in this book are the author's own,
and may not necessarily reflect those of the IPD.

Quotation on p.10 printed with kind
permission of Pearson Education Ltd.

INSTITUTE OF PERSONNEL
AND DEVELOPMENT

IPD House, Camp Road, Wimbledon, London SW19 4UX
Tel: 020-8971-9000   Fax: 020-8263-3333
Registered office as above. Registered Charity No. 1038333
A company limited by guarantee. Registered in England No. 2931892

Contents

Acknowledgements

Many people and organisations have contributed to this book, either by way of formal contributions or through informal discussion. Special thanks are due to Richard Goff of IPD Enterprises for his editorial input and words of encouragement. I should also like to express my grateful thanks to the following personnel who willingly gave their time to answer my questions: Lesley Ball of Asda Stores, Morag McLeod of Philips Research Laboratories, and Andy Gilbert of Career Strategies Ltd.

Publisher's acknowledgements

IPD Publications gratefully acknowledges the help and expertise of Zella King of Birkbeck College, University of London, who wrote the IPD Guide *Career Management in Organisations* (London, IPD, 1998), the original inspiration for this book.

Other titles in the series

Glossary

Career	The total sequence of employment-related positions, roles, activities and experiences encountered by an individual.
Career action centre	A drop-in centre with open access to such resources as literature, videos and CD-ROMs, and information about financial and educational support.
Career bridges	Circumstances that facilitate individuals moving into new areas of experience, usually in cross-functional moves.
Career coaching	As career counselling, but including directive feedback and training in career-related skills.
Career counselling	Impartial advice provided on a one-to-one basis to an individual about his or her capabilities and career options, often by a qualified counsellor who is external to the organisation.
Career development	The process of assessing, aligning and balancing organisational and individual needs, capabilities, opportunities and challenges through multiple

approaches and methods. It empha- sises the person as an individual who performs, configures and adapts vari- ous work roles. Its major intervention is self-assessment and developmental processes that affect individual and organisational abilities to generate optimal matches of people and jobs (Tracey, 1991[1]).

Career direction
The main type of occupation followed by an individual.

Career goal
The career end-result that an individ- ual hopes to achieve (cf *Career objective*) (Reynolds *et al*, 1997).

Career ladder
A carefully sequenced series of jobs from the lowest to the highest level (in terms of responsibilities, rewards and challenges) within an organisational function.

Career management
Systematically preparing, implement- ing and monitoring of an individual's career plan. It may be driven by the individual, the organisation, or both (Reynolds *et al*, 1997).

Career objective
A specific career step that an individ- ual hopes to achieve within a prede- termined time (cf *Career goal*) (Reynolds *et al*, 1997).

Career path
The actual sequence of jobs that an individual follows.

Career perspective (individual) An individual's needs, desires and short- and long-term priorities for his or her career, determined by his or her previous experiences, capabilities, family situation, financial commitments, lifestyle choices and future plans.

Career perspective (organisation) An organisation's needs and priorities for individual jobs and the development of its employees, determined by strategic objectives.

Career-planning The process of establishing short- or long-term career goals and objectives and defining the specific steps required to achieve them (Tracey, 1991). These steps may include the types of job, training, development and other activities.

Career plateau Reaching a dead-end in an organisation with no prospects of further promotion. It may occur because of a shortage of more senior positions or because individuals are viewed as having exhausted their potential.

Career workshops Provide individuals with time away from the workplace to review their skills, knowledge and aspirations and help in planning how to realise their career goals.

Competency	An observable skill or ability to complete tasks successfully.
Development centres	A scheduled group session, run by an external facilitator and/or a member of the organisation, to identify individuals' development and training needs.
Development roles/positions	Short-term positions, often involving projects and assignments, used to enhance individuals' knowledge, skills and abilities. The positions are generally ones where an individual with transferable skills and potential can make, with managerial support, an early contribution.
Job-posting	Open advertising of job opportunities within an organisation.
Mentor	A senior member of the organisation or a colleague who provides advice and guidance and who may also act as a protector, advocate or sponsor.
Networking	The effective initiation and maintenance of social relationships for career-related purposes (Arnold, 1997).[2]
Outplacement	A programme of advisory facilities and resources provided to individuals leaving an organisation in order to help them clarify and implement plans for the future.

Personal development plan (PDP)	A statement of how an individual's skills and knowledge might develop, for the achievement of which the individual takes primary responsibility.
Portfolio career	This applies to individuals who seek out developmental experiences and job moves in order to enhance and update their skill profiles, thereby keeping pace with the rapid changes in roles and demands.
Potential	The capability to do a bigger and/or broader job at some time in the future.
Psychological contract	An individual's belief regarding the (unwritten) agreement that he or she has with the employer about what he or she will contribute to the employer, and what he or she can expect in return.
Secondment	A job move where the individual leaves his or her main job or function temporarily but maintains a 'home link'.
Self-assessment	Reflection by individuals on their 'performance' using a range of methods including tests, questionnaires, individual or group exercises, feedback from observers and discussions with managers, mentors, counsellors and

	peers. The aim is to identify strengths and developmental needs.
Self-development	Personal development, with the individual taking primary responsibility for his or her own learning and for choosing the means to achieve this (Pedler *et al*, 1986).
Succession-planning	The planned replacement of individuals within the organisation.

End-notes

1 Reprinted from *Human Resources Glossary* by William R. Tracey. Copyright © 1991 AMACOM, a division of American Management Association International. Reprinted by permission of AMACOM, a division of American Management Association International, New York, NY. All rights reserved. http://www.amenet.org.

2 Reprinted by permission of Paul Chapman Publishing Ltd From J. Arnold, *Managing Careers into the 21st Century*, © J. Arnold 1997.

What is the purpose of this guide and who should read it?

Introduction

Much has been written about the changing nature of organisations and the death of the traditional career. In other words, individuals can no longer expect job security and a career path that takes them through a steady progression of jobs of increasing status and responsibility. So should employers bother to invest in career development when many of their employees will leave to pursue their career goals and objectives elsewhere?

It is true that there has been a fundamental shift in the nature of careers both from the individual and organisational viewpoints. Many people expect to work for a number of employers, perhaps in differing functions, during their working lives. However, employers should not use this as an excuse for failing to invest in career development or concentrating on the development of high-flyers only. The mission statements of many organisations stress that 'Our people are our main asset' but are not backed up by integrated systems that seek to develop employees to realise their full potential. In this book we propose that organisations seek to attract, retain and develop *all* their employees, regardless of their likely length of service. They need to balance the long-term interventions required for successful career development with the short-term pushes required to achieve performance targets. Only in this way can organisational goals be realised.

Purpose and objectives

This book is intended to provide a good-practice guide to employers seeking to develop their employees' careers. It does not ignore the changing nature of work but aims to help employers to recognise and deal with the future shape and context of careers.

We consider the changing nature of careers, the effect this has on career development, and the advantages of an integrated approach. We also look at a number of career development interventions and provide guidance on a practical approach to implementation. Finally, the special provisions that may be necessary for certain groups of worker are covered.

Our objectives are to enable readers to:

- understand career development from the perspective of the individual employee as well as that of the organisation, and to reconcile those perspectives

- acquire the tools necessary to review existing career development practices and to make plans to design and implement new career development interventions.

Who should read this guide?

This book is concerned with career development by and within organisations and has been written from the viewpoint of the organisation. We do stress, however, the need to take account of the individual perspective. This is because careers are subjective as well as objective, ie 'success' depends on the individual's interpretation of events as well as other people's views. So, in managing and developing careers within organisations, it is vital that the views of the individual are taken into account and that decisions are based on satisfying the needs of both parties in the employment relationship.

This book is aimed at anyone with responsibility for devising or implementing career development strategies in organisations. This may include line managers, personnel and development (P&D) professionals, non-specialists whose responsibilities include personnel management (eg administrative staff in small organisations), mentors, coaches and career counsellors. The book should also prove useful, however, to individuals seeking to make career plans and to students on business and personnel management programmes.

Best practice

We aim to provide best-practice guidelines, but it is worth bearing in mind that there is no single best-practice

3

approach to career development, because organisational contexts vary so dramatically. A number of interventions are explored and readers are given advice on how to select the best strategy for their own organisation. This depends on their circumstances and the career objectives of the individuals concerned.

What is a career?

- ✔ A changing definition
- ✔ Individual and organisational perspectives
- ✔ The changing context
- ✔ The psychological contract
- ✔ The future shape of careers

A changing definition

The career is a relatively recent concept which resulted from the growth of organisations during the twentieth century. It implies some form of competition, where the winners are deemed to have beaten the opposition when they gain promotion and progress further up the managerial hierarchy.

Traditionally the term 'career' has implied a series of upward moves with steadily increasing responsibility, status and rewards. Thus 'having a successful career' is the province of an élite few (and then only for the period of time that they are considered to have the potential for the next move). Further, many would view careers as relevant only to managerial or professional positions and, if career success is to be achieved within one organisation, probably applicable only to larger organisations.

Nowadays organisations and society have changed to such an extent that people no longer expect or, in many cases, even want a long-term career within a single organisation. They are more concerned with their own development in terms of updating their skills and knowledge. They may achieve this not just by upward progression within one organisation but by lateral moves, broader work experience and moves to other organisations and across different types of employment, including self-employment. As a consequence, the focus of career development has shifted from assessing employees' potential for promotion towards realising their potential via role adaptation and flexibility, projects and teamworking, development positions and lateral job movements.

We need therefore to broaden the definition of 'career' to encompass the personal development that results from work experience for all individuals. So the definition of a career that we shall be using in this book comes from the *IPD Guide on Career Management in Organisations* (1998, vii):

> The total sequence of employment-related positions, roles, activities and experiences encountered by an individual.

Individual and organisational perspectives

What do individuals want from their careers? The answers obviously vary and depend on a number of factors:

- capabilities
- previous experience
- current position

- age
- domestic circumstances
- financial situation
- lifestyle choices
- plans for the future.

The choices that individuals make are determined by these factors and the perceived opportunities at a particular point in time. For example, a retired chief executive may be very happy to undertake part-time lecturing at a local further education college when only five years previously he or she was still striving to climb the corporate ladder and would never have considered such a position.

Organisations, on the other hand, manage their resourcing activities to ensure that (to borrow a well-known phrase) 'the right people with the right skills are in the right place at the right time to achieve strategic objectives'. The nature of the industry in question and the changes it is undergoing will be prime factors in determining how jobs are structured, the characteristics that are sought in potential applicants (internal and external) and applicants' developmental needs.

These two perspectives necessarily impinge on each other. A dialogue between the two parties to the employment relationship is therefore essential, so that each is aware of the needs and expectations of the other. Further, the dialogue must be a continuous one, so that changes affecting either perspective are also clearly communicated. For instance, a part-time employee may be interested in moving to a full-time position within a department because of changed family circumstances. This employee may simply wait for a suitable vacancy to arise, unaware that the departmental manager is making radical plans to redistribute workloads in preparation for an imminent restructuring programme.

The changing context

Careers are being transformed by the following:

- social changes, eg trends relating to the demographic composition of the workforce
- economic changes, eg rapid growth of the global market-place, increased competition, the shift of employment from the manufacturing to the service sector, and the fact that most emerging new firms employ fewer than 20 people
- organisation-culture changes resulting from changes of ownership, legislation and regulations, and internal innovative pressures
- technological changes, eg the automation of formerly labour-intensive processes, the effect on communications, and the growth of associated industries and employment.

Let's look at some of these changes in more detail. Undoubtedly the composition of the workforce is changing in the UK: the numbers of men and women in the labour market are now almost equal, there are more dual-career households, there is a greater ethnic mix and the average age of the workforce is increasing. There is also a more varied range of contracts on offer, including part-time, temporary, fixed-term, job-sharing, homeworking and contracts for service. (See Appendix 1 for more details.)

There have been changes in the demand for particular skills due to the shift in the UK away from its manufacturing base to service provision. Difficulties in filling vacancies for information technology (IT) and call-centre staff are common occurrences, whereas unemployment is more likely for people possessing traditional skills that are fast becoming obsolete. Another paradox is that, while the demand for managerial, technical and professional staff is expected to continue to rise, many of the other new jobs on offer are part-time and low paid, often involving significant de-skilling. Further, many highly skilled or 'knowledge' workers such as IT specialists and consultants, tend to choose, despite a high demand for their services, to remain on the outside of mainstream organisational life on contracts of service rather than contracts of employment. The advantage to them is that this enables them to exert greater control over their working lives and earn more money.

The trend towards flatter structures in organisations has often been cited as the main reason for the demise of the traditional career. Traditional career ladders are under threat in the leaner, flatter and more flexible organisations that have resulted from downsizing, de-layering and the devolution of duties. It is worth pointing out that hierarchies do still exist, but the steps between levels are steeper and promotion is therefore more difficult to gain.

A leading commentator, Charles Handy, predicted that organisations would move towards a 'clover-leaf' organisation, compromising a small core of permanent staff with roughly equal proportions of subcontracted work and temporary workers, thus involving new forms of more flexible contracts. There is dissent over the extent to which this has occurred but in some ways this prediction has been realised: the IT consultants mentioned above, for instance, would be an example of subcontracted workers.

These changes in the nature of work will inevitably have implications for the way in which organisations undertake to structure jobs and develop the careers of their employees:

> There is an increase in managerial roles with a stronger focus on teamworking and the use of flexible contracts. Managerial jobs in themselves tend to be less specific and have a stronger project dimension. Furthermore, the trend towards empowerment means that the nature of the managerial role has changed. Managers must now act as resource providers and diplomats rather than those who command and control. Self-directed teams also further undermine the traditional managerial role.

> Pemberton, Refausse and Evans, 1998

In summary, we are now seeing the emergence of new organisational structures and changes in the nature of work, with more emphasis on projects and teamworking and less clearly defined roles. In turn there has been a shift in the skills mix required of employees, and this has implications for contracts of employment.

The psychological contract

The traditional career was based on mutual interests and a balance of obligations between the employer and employee. The terms of this relationship were described not only in the formal contract of employment but also in the unwritten psychological contract – the understanding that both parties have about what is expected from the other and what will be delivered in return. Carole Pemberton (1998, 11) sets out a career model of typical obligations and expectations, applicable up until the 1980s, reproduced here on page 12.

This traditional career contract relied heavily on the future being reasonably predictable. The fast pace of continuous change now facing organisations means that there is much more uncertainty about the future, which necessarily affects the organisation's ability to fulfil the obligations set out above. Further, as we have previously stated, individuals expect that their working lives will involve more frequent changes in job, employer and skills requirements than previously.

What does this mean for the psychological contract? In the new career context, employers need to compensate for the reduced security of employment by offering employees financial and non-financial rewards, including the opportunity to develop themselves and increase their employability. The employer will expect employees to increase their output and enhance their skills, as well as remaining loyal and committed, even if only in the short term.

Thus the balance of power seems to have shifted even more towards the employer. Employees certainly seem to be working longer hours, with unwanted additional responsibilities, under more pressure to achieve stringent targets and with more limited prospects of promotion than before. Not surprisingly the motivation and commitment of employees has been hard to sustain following major changes, especially where employees have not been offered development opportunities.

In fact the response of many organisations has been to

Career model

I offer...	The organisation expects...
● my loyalty ● in-depth knowledge of this organisation ● acceptance of bureaucratic systems which will define my rate of progress ● a willingness to go beyond the call of duty when required	● loyalty ● staff with a deep understanding of how business is done here ● a willingness to build a career slowly through a defined system ● an 'organisation man' who puts the organisation before outside interests
I expect...	**The organisation offers...**
● to have job security ● regular pay increases ● recognition for length of time given ● to have my experience taken account of	● job security ● regular pay increases based on length of service, rather than performance measures ● status and rewards for length of service ● respect for experience

promote career 'self-management' or 'self-development', shifting the responsibility to the individual but without providing the necessary facilitative mechanisms of support. For instance, self-motivated individuals may decide that they need to broaden their skills but find there is no encouragement or opportunity for, say, secondments to other departments, work shadowing of more senior staff, or involvement in project teams.

The traditional psychological contract was often said to be 'relational', ie an exchange of long-term security for loyalty. Nowadays, the contract is more 'transactional', ie based on a more explicit negotiation between the two parties regarding expectations and obligations. To sum up, the trend is from a traditional 'job for life' approach towards a 'job for now' attitude.

The future shape of careers

We have covered many of the recent changes mentioned above. It is true that traditional careers have not disappeared altogether, especially for managerial and professional roles, but in the future we shall see a greater incidence of:

- movements in and out of organisations, and from large to smaller enterprises
- lateral job moves
- role adaptation
- assignment and project work
- changes in career direction
- moves from full-time 'permanent' employment to periods of temporary, part-time and casual work and/or unemployment

- moves from employment to self-employment
- 'portfolio careers' (to use Charles Handy's term), ie those comprising a number of the above experiences. Such moves may be self-driven or forced by outside circumstances, but by and large portfolio workers seek out developmental experiences in order to enhance and update their skills profiles.

In summary, careers are nowadays much more broadly defined than before, with the emphasis less on employment and more on employability and 'career resilience'. Consequently individuals should seek to gain competitive and up-to-date skills to help them find acceptable work as and when required. But does this mean that managers should abdicate all responsibility for career development, because there are no guarantees that employees will stay? As Waterman, Waterman and Collard (1994, 87) put it:

> How can an enterprise build capabilities, forge empowered teams, develop a deep understanding of its customers, and – most important – create a sense of community or common purpose unless it has a relationship with its employees based on mutual trust and caring? And how can an enterprise build such a relationship unless it commits something to employees and employees commit something to it?

The responsibility for developing careers and thereby maintaining individuals' employability should be a shared one between the employer and the employee.

Finally, in line with our redefining the notion of a career, we are also seeing greater diversity among views on 'career success'. This partly follows from feelings of job insecurity, real or perceived, and has led many individuals to rethink their career priorities. The finding of the *IPD Guide* (1998, 8) was that:

> Some may still aspire to high positions within corporate hierarchies. Others may be most concerned to underwrite their job security by gaining a reputation for their skills and expertise. Some people may be concerned with having autonomy and independence in their work life, or achieving a meaningful balance so that work becomes neither too dominating nor too boring. Others may seek continuing growth and challenge through a variety of work roles.
>
> People may be less willing to sacrifice personal interests, activities and relationships to employing organisations which can no longer offer them security or promotion prospects, unless the employer offers something else in return. Career self-management for some will be about doing everything they can to work their way to the top of their organisation or profession. For others it may be about managing their performance at work to meet their employer's needs while safeguarding the quality of their personal life. Or about seeking out opportunities to develop a range of skills that could be used at a later date in another context, such as to set up their own business.

What is career development?

- ☑ Definitions of terms
- ☑ Principles of learning and development
- ☑ Who is responsible?
- ☑ The personnel/line-management relationship
- ☑ Conclusion

Definitions of terms

The terms 'career development' and 'career management' tend to be used interchangeably by commentators and practitioners. Consequently there was some debate as to which term was the more appropriate for this book. There are obviously many similarities between the two processes, but the term 'career development' was chosen because, as defined below, it implies the need to balance organisational and individual needs and the range of interventions that are available.

We shall be using a definition of career development supplied by *The Human Resources Glossary* (Tracey, 1991, 43):

> The process of assessing, aligning and balancing organisational and individual needs, capabilities,

opportunities and challenges through multiple approaches and methods. It emphasises the person as an individual who performs, configures and adapts various work roles. Its major intervention is self-assessment and developmental processes that affect individual and organisational abilities to generate optimal matches of people and jobs.

On the other hand, the *Dictionary of HRD* (Reynolds, Sambrook and Stewart 1997, 27) provides a somewhat narrower definition for career management:

Systematically preparing, implementing and monitoring an individual's career plan. It may be driven by the individual, or the organisation, or both.

With these definitions in mind, we shall, when using the term 'career development', also be referring to career management from the organisational perspective.

As a final comparison, a definition of 'career-planning' is provided below (Tracey, 1991, 43). Here the emphasis is on the need for this process to be driven by the individual:

The process of establishing short- or long-term career goals and objectives and defining the specific steps required to achieve them.

These steps may include the types of job, training, development and other activities. You may wish to refer to the glossary at the front of this book for definitions of a number of related terms.

Let's now consider some principles of learning and development.

Principles of learning and development

When asked to list the major milestones in their career development, most people will cite a particular task or project, an unexpected job move or promotion – ie some kind of work experience. But how can the information absorbed from such experience be put to good use? Charles Jackson (1996, 262–3) states that:

> the challenge for individuals and organisations is how best to develop careers. For employers this means formulating and delivering strategies that will harness the potential and develop the skills of *all* their employees. For individuals it means dealing with more complexity in career choices and developing the skills to manage career transitions. For both parties it means having a clear understanding of the role of learning and development activities.

> © Institute for Employment Studies 1996
> (See Jackson 1996)

Jackson (1996, 262–3) says that learning and development should be organised on the following principles:

1   most development takes place in the workplace rather than on external training courses
2   development activities are best delivered by work colleagues and line managers
3   development focuses on future job skills as much as on the current job
4   training and development activities for individuals and organisations have a clear purpose, order of priority and sense of direction

5   training and development proactively anticipates future organisational requirements
6   genuine equality of opportunity is achieved by opening up options for learning and development to all employees.

© Institute for Employment Studies 1996
(See Jackson 1996)

It is clear that there is a need for careful planning of training and development activities in order for them to be successfully translated into useful learning experiences.

Who is responsible?

To use the terminology of Hirsh and Jackson (1996), up until the late 1980s to early 1990s organisations engaging in career development adopted an approach that could best be described as a 'leave-it-to-us' or paternalistic one. One of its features was that larger organisations tended to run their career development programmes centrally, concentrating in the main on management development and succession-planning. Individuals would be regularly consulted to ensure that information on their career aspirations was up to date, but their role was largely reactive. Employees entrusted major decisions affecting their careers to the organisation, often simply waiting for the employer to bring a promotion opportunity to their attention (and running the risk of stalling their careers within the organisation if they turned promotion down).

After this period there was a big swing towards an 'over-to-you' approach, in which interventions were aimed at getting employees to manage their own careers. The organisation's role became, in theory, one of providing a supportive environment, but this rarely occurred. The view that prevailed was that an integrated and systematic approach to career development was no longer necessary and that initiatives such as rewarding performance would be sufficient. Further, there was a shift towards including the whole workforce, not just selected groups, and the provisions, such as they were, tended to be provided locally rather than centrally.

This change in emphasis inevitably led to problems. Alan Mumford (1988) found in his research that even top managers were finding that their learning and development was unplanned, disorganised and did not encourage reflection. Further, self-managed career development was unlikely to ensure the achievement of business objectives, because there was no attempt to link them together.

There were obvious drawbacks to both approaches and the main interventions applicable to them are laid out in the table on page 22.

Not surprisingly we have recently seen a further shift in emphasis, and many organisations now advocate a 'we're-in-it-together' or partnership approach. Here the self-development processes introduced in the 'over-to-you' phase are still valued but sit alongside a strong emphasis on succession-planning and senior management development. Nowadays these latter two interventions are being played out in less predictable circumstances and are therefore shorter-term processes. Further, they do not just concentrate on high-flyers, and are a shared management activity rather than an 'ivory tower' responsibility. Finally, there is more willingness to take into account individuals' aspirations and circumstances in the succession-planning process.

Career development interventions

Leave-it-to-us	Over-to-you
Centralised succession planning	Personal development plans (PDPs)
Emphasis on management development	Career action centres (CACs)
Graduate recruitment programme	Development centres (DCs)
Training and development activities initiated by the organisation	Career workshops
Performance appraisal scheme controlled by P&D	Networking
Counselling provision	Career counselling

You have probably guessed that in this book we shall be advocating a shared responsibility for career development, ie a partnership approach. Individuals must take responsibility for their own careers, but they need their employer to ensure that the environment is a supportive one and that barriers to career development are dismantled.

The personnel/line-management relationship

We discussed above the responsibility for career development lying with the organisation, the individual or both. But who are we actually referring to when we talk about the 'organisation's responsibility'? Are career development interventions a P&D or line-management responsibility?

The answer, as you might expect, is not a simple one. Alongside the shifts in responsibility described above we have also seen changes in the respective roles of P&D professionals and line managers. In many cases this has resulted from restructuring, leading to the decentralisation of P&D activities and a devolution of people-management responsibilities to the line.

In any event, line managers are clearly and primarily responsible for the development of their staff (though many do not award this sufficient priority). They have a role to play in, for example:

- appraising performance
- identifying training and development needs
- reviewing progress and achievement of objectives
- reviewing career development and potential
- involving others in staff development, eg specialists and colleagues
- looking for development opportunities and facilitating their implementation
- delegating tasks for development purposes
- demonstrating good practice, ie acting as a role model
- leading pre- and post-training and development activity reviews
- budgeting for training and development costs
- allowing risk-taking
- awarding performance related pay (PRP) against objective criteria
- keeping staff up to date on achievements and difficulties at departmental and corporate levels.

In their 'new' supportive roles P&D specialists can help line managers with many of these activities, such as identifying training and development needs, managing on-the-job learning, following up appraisal action points and determining reward.

Conclusion

In summary, career development is more than centralised succession-planning and the use of management and graduate development programmes to encourage high-flyers. Organisations will always need their 'solid citizens' to help them to achieve their corporate objectives and, because the working population is an ageing one, they cannot afford to ignore the needs and aspirations of all their employees, regardless of age. Further, the changing nature of work will mean a continuous need for (re)education and (re)training, and this is associated with government-led initiatives concerning lifelong learning.

Why do organisations need career development?

The disadvantages of not engaging in career development

There is an argument that says that, because of the demise of traditional careers, it is pointless to invest in career development. Supporters of this view point to the following reasons:

- People expect to have several different employers during their working lives, so investment in their development would be a waste of money.
- When injections of skill and expertise are needed by organisations they can simply poach from other employers or buy in the required talent in the form of consultants or fixed-term appointments.

- 'Cream will always rise to the top', ie the high-flyers who have ability, drive and ambition will manage their own careers and achieve the results required at the appropriate time, without the need for 'hand-holding' by the employer.
- For other, more dispensable, employees, job-related training is all that is necessary to achieve performance in the 'job-for-now' approach to employment.

This all seems to be logical and practical, but there are several disadvantages for organisations choosing not to get involved in developing the careers of their staff:

- The UK already lags behind many of its international competitors in terms of the educational attainments of its workforce. Though initiatives such as National Vocational Qualifications (NVQs), the Management Charter Initiative (MCI) and Investors in People (IiP) have been launched to encourage vocational training, comparisons with such countries as Germany, France and Holland are still unfavourable.
- Frustration over a perceived lack of development opportunities will lead to increased labour turnover and the associated costs of replacement, ie covering vacancies as well as hiring, inducting and training new recruits.
- Employees who are demotivated may well underperform and are unlikely to develop more than a small percentage of their true potential.
- Demographic changes may make it difficult to readily hire people with the appropriate skills and

knowledge, so more time will have to be spent on job design and human resource planning.

- Good-quality candidates may decide not to apply for vacancies if they are aware of probable limitations on career development opportunities in the organisation.
- Downsizing, de-layering and devolution may lead to resentment on the part of employees who see that their workload and responsibility have increased but that their promotion prospects have diminished or even disappeared. This will inevitably affect motivation, commitment and performance.
- An absence of development initiatives encouraging lateral moves, cross-functional secondments and assignment-based work will increase the frustration felt by plateaued managers. Further, an organisational culture that does not positively promote and support such moves will find that they are resisted or only reluctantly accepted.
- Failure to get managers involved in developing the careers of their staff results in missed opportunities to develop the managers themselves, as well as in closing potential lines of communication across the organisation which would cut across hierarchical boundaries.
- A lack of knowledge about employees' skills, knowledge and career aspirations will mean that many staff may suffer from the 'square pegs in round holes' syndrome. Again, this will have a detrimental effect on their performance and, ultimately, that of the organisation.

The advantages of a structured approach

People develop through a combination of training and experience, the latter being by far the more important. As we have already stated, much valuable learning does result from unplanned and unforeseen experiences, but organisations should not be prepared to leave the management of experience to chance.

The advantages of investing in career development are many. The IPD Guide (1998, pp ix–x) provides the following examples:

- A frank exchange of mutual expectations at the recruitment stage can reduce later wastage rates and lost investment in training and development, as well as helping to attract the right applicants.
- Such an exchange enables a coherent understanding of opportunities and expectations between the organisation and the individual to be developed over time.
- It also facilitates the alignment of individual and organisation perspectives and enables individuals' skills and knowledge to be used more effectively.
- It assists managers to manage change, including situations in which individuals' career perspectives and expectations are adversely affected.
- The contribution made towards improving motivation, flexibility and commitment in the workforce will positively affect productivity, costs and labour turnover.
- It assists in the retention of key skills.

- Training and development effort should be more effectively focused.

In summary, the result of all the above factors should result in a positive effect on the bottom line.

Motivational issues

Much has been written about which factors in the workplace are motivational ones. We do not intend here to open up the theoretical debate, but do acknowledge that different factors motivate different people at different times. The *Employment in Britain* survey (Guest, 1995) throws some light onto this complex subject and provides information about what people want from work. Over 70 per cent of those questioned felt that the following four sets of factors were essential or very important:

- the type of work which they are doing, the opportunity to use their initiative and abilities whilst at work – in effect, to be stretched in terms of problem-solving and creativity
- job security
- working with friendly and supportive people; having a good relationship with their supervisor
- good pay and satisfactory physical working conditions.

So we are assuming in this book that regular promotions are generally accepted to be motivational and that a failure to invest in career development will have an adverse impact on levels of motivation and commitment in the workplace.

How can organisations seek to attract and retain high-quality people when they are no longer able to offer them a progressively upwardly mobile career or even long-term employment? Commentators seem to agree that there are alternatives to promotion, but these must provide challenge and autonomy and be suitably rewarded. (See Chapter 5 for more details of the choices available.)

The need for integration

Career development interventions must be integrated both vertically and horizontally within the organisation. This means that they must be designed to contribute to organisational success (vertical integration) and to 'fit' with or support other P&D activities (horizontal integration). If sufficient attention is not paid to these requirements, then the various activities chosen may contradict each other or pull in different directions. Here are some examples of the kind of dilemma that can result:

- In a de-layered environment, managers are under increased pressure to get the work done and to meet performance targets, but they have fewer staff than previously to achieve this. They therefore lack the time and resources to be able to offer development opportunities.
- Performance appraisal schemes often serve several purposes, such as assessing current performance, reviewing future development and determining reward. Employees may be unwilling to admit to developmental needs in case doing so has a detrimental effect on performance-related pay.
- Where managers wish to facilitate lateral and cross-functional job moves for their staff, the

individuals concerned may resist such initiatives if there is an insufficient level of trust and if the organisational culture does not appear to 'value' this approach.

- Payment systems are traditionally geared to rewarding progress and status within the organisation. Where organisations are striving to achieve continuous improvements, individuals may be encouraged to increase their knowledge and skills (or competencies) but be dismayed to find that the reward mechanism has not been changed to reflect this change in emphasis.

It is clear that career development interventions must support and be supported by other important P&D activities, notably:

- recruitment and selection
- human resource planning
- succession-planning
- training and development
- management development
- reward
- performance management.

Career development interventions can also assist in such areas as organisation design, communications and cultural changes. A fully integrated system would entail the gearing of all these activities towards the achievement of organisational goals.

Legislation

There is no specific right to career development for employees, but there are related rights in equal access to opportunities for promotion, transfer and training, to study leave for young people and to information about personal data. Further, these rights are beginning to extend beyond core employees, and new rights are emerging for those working elsewhere in the EU, part-timers and other 'workers'. (See Appendix 2 for further details.)

What do we mean by career development interventions?

Variety of approaches

It is not our intention here to prescribe one model or best-practice approach to career development. You need to decide what your purposes are in embarking on a career development programme and adopt a variety of interventions that best fit your circumstances and culture. You also need to take account of the career goals and objectives of your employees, as well as considering their vertical and horizontal integration with other organisational activities.

The information given below on a number of these interventions should assist you in making this judgement. (Further guidance is given in Chapter 6.)

The interventions chosen may vary in approach:

- *Formal v informal* – career workshops and development centres are examples of formal (off-the-job) approaches, whereas encouraging individuals to self-manage their careers may be largely informal (and take place as part of day-to-day work activities).
- *Centralised v local provisions* – succession-planning and annual appraisal schemes are generally monitored and organised centrally, whereas coaching is largely a line-manager activity provided at the local level.
- *The language chosen* – ie how do organisations refer to the capabilities of their employees? Some may choose a combination of knowledge, skills, attitudes and experience, but many others use competencies as the common language binding all their P and D processes together.
- *The workers covered* – we advocate throughout this book that career development programmes should apply to all employees, but organisations may decide that some interventions are appropriate only for certain groups. For instance, the extension of an organisation's mentoring programme beyond graduate entrants to other groups of workers might be deemed to be potentially beneficial but too cumbersome to administer, and expensive. Further, in using the term 'workers' above, our intention was to raise

the question as to whether career development processes are applicable to core employees only or whether the organisation would benefit from the inclusion of wider groups, such as flexible workers. (See Chapter 7 for more information on this aspect.)

Purposes of career development interventions

Charles Jackson *et al* (1996, 36) identifies five purposes, applying equally to the individual and the organisation:

1   assessment – activities to provide the individual and organisation with the opportunity to learn about individuals' strengths, weaknesses, interests etc
2   career options – activities to assist individuals' and their managers' understanding of current and future career and job options
3   action-planning – planning of specific, concrete, time-based learning activities by individuals and organisations
4   skill development – activities to promote or deliver skill development
5   vacancy-filling – activities designed to manage the internal labour market in line with business needs and organisational culture.

Jackson *et al* (1996, 37) show pictorially how organisations can use a variety of interventions to deliver these purposes. (The majority of these interventions are commented on below.)

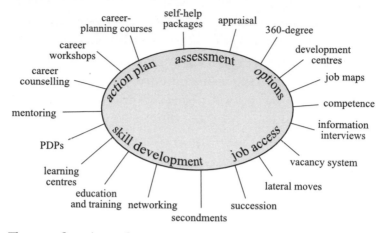

The core functions of career development

Example interventions

There are many categorisations of activities or methods that could be deemed part of a career development programme. In some instances – eg recruitment, reward, human resource planning, training and performance appraisal – it is arguable that these are key P&D activities in their own right. As we stated in Chapter 4, career development must be integrated with these activities to ensure that each supports the other in the drive to achieve organisational goals. For instance, organisations may decide to revise their existing performance appraisal scheme and introduce 360-degree feedback to assist individuals in identifying where their strengths lie and which areas require development.

With this in mind, we shall concentrate below on a number of interventions that organisations may choose as part of their career development programme. This is not intended to be a definitive list but gives a taste of the range of interventions available, along with their pros and cons. (The Glossary on pages viii–xiii provides further definitions of some of these terms.)

Before commencing our examination, however, we need first to remind you of two important processes underlying career development: they are self-development and self-assessment, and both will be encouraged by most of the interventions listed below. Another important feature to include is a two-way dialogue, so that decisions are made only when the needs and wishes of both parties are taken into account.

Succession-planning

This concerns the planned replacement of individuals within an organisation. It may focus on one particular job, eg the chief executive's, extend to all senior management positions or, increasingly nowadays, include all posts considered crucial to the organisation's day-to-day effectiveness. Usually a centralised task carried out by senior personnel, it enables an organisation to plan the strategic development and deployment of staff over time. The main advantage is that the replacement of key staff may be effected with minimum disruption and without incurring the high costs of seeking external replacements. The disadvantages are that succession planning is still considered to be an élitist process concerned with management and graduate development only and, if it is not an open and transparent system, that it may be viewed as contradictory to other interventions such as job-posting.

To be successful in today's climate succession-planning should not be a central function but a *shared* management activity. Further, it should concentrate less on individual positions, ie 'the crown princes', and more on the pools of personnel needed to fulfil future job roles. Competency frameworks are useful here, because they aim to identify the core competencies that the organisation wishes to develop in order to meet its goals.

Job-posting or internal vacancy notification

There are many disadvantages to encounter when organisations simply appoint individuals to vacant posts without advertising. The two prime concerns are these:

- From an equal opportunities point of view, this is a dubious practice.
- The organisation is missing an opportunity to improve its information base regarding employees' skills and aspirations.

If organisations move to a system whereby all vacancies are advertised internally, possibly in advance of external advertising, then this practice will support other self development initiatives, and individuals will be more willing to nominate themselves. (Please note that we are not suggesting that organisations only advertise internally to the exclusion of external sources of new recruits, because this might also have equal opportunities implications.)

Development centres (DCs)

DCs use such techniques as job simulations, role plays and presentations to assess the capabilities (or competencies) and development needs of existing employees.

There are many different forms of DC, so there is some confusion over the term. Whiddett and Hollyforde (1999, 109) distinguish between the terms 'assessment centres' (for selection purposes) and 'development centres' (for participants to practise and get feedback on competencies). For career development purposes, they introduce the term 'assessment for development centres' (ADCs) to identify what an individual would have to learn, or improve on, to be considered a suitable candidate for another job.

The reception given by participants to DCs or ADCs has not always been favourable: some view them as filtering mechanisms to exclude candidates from promotion or development, rather than the reverse. If introduced at a time of disruption within an organisation, they can even be viewed as mechanisms for redundancy selection. In response to such criticisms, the Roffey Park Management Institute has devised a Personal Exploration and Evaluation Review (Peer) Centre to help people to maximise their

---

Case-study 1: NHS Career Development Register

In recognition of the underrepresentation of women in the top echelons of the health service, the NHS Career Development Register commissioned Roffey Park Management Institute to run a Peer Centre for a group of senior women managers. This was duly carried out. Linda Holbeche (1995, 28) reports that feedback has so far been good, one chief executive describing the experience of the Peer Centre as 'helpful to me personally and, I believe, to many of my colleagues'. The process did not stop there, however, for a number of other interventions were used to follow up the specific needs of individuals. These included one-to-one career coaching, specialist training (such as management and business leadership courses), an action learning management development initiative, and DC attendance.

---

potential. The focus here is very much on personal development, the participants running many of the assessment
processes themselves. Staff at the centre provide support for
participants to formulate a personal development plan
(PDP), but the participants own the results and feedback.

Personal Development Plans (PDPs)

PDPs may result from a number of sources, such as DCs, or
from the performance appraisal process. A PDP is a developmental action plan aimed at enhancing skills and knowledge, for which the individual takes primary responsibility.
Difficulties arise when individuals do not feel comfortable
enough to be honest about their developmental needs. John
Arnold (1997, 5) sums up the dilemma:

> A tightrope has to be walked between on the one
> hand having PDPs that are very detached from the
> organisation's HR processes and on the other hand
> having PDPs closely scrutinised by members of
> management. The former line invites a reaction of
> 'Why bother?' from potential PDP users, whilst the
> latter takes ownership away from individuals and
> turns PDPs into another management tool.[1]

Career Action Centres (CACs)

CACs are often referred to as learning resource centres and
are essentially drop-in centres where a variety of career-
related services is available. This may include literature,
videos and computer-based packages for self-assessment
purposes, as well as access to counselling advice on job-
hunting skills, networking and career information. Difficulties arise when individuals are torn between the need to

take time away from the workplace to concentrate on their long-term developmental needs and the more immediate demands of their jobs. This may be compounded by the mixed messages they receive concerning their employer's stated commitment to their self-development and the pressure to work long hours and to increase outputs. The result can be that CACs, which are expensive to run, are seriously under-used or are associated only with outplacement services. (See Case-study 3.)

Career workshops and seminars

CACs may also provide the location for, or access to, career workshops and seminars, usually run by impartial facilitators. Here information, exercises and resources are provided that aid career-planning and decision-making. The emphasis is on self-development and, where individuals are not used to this approach, those individuals may resist this type of initiative. The reason for the workshops/seminars must therefore be carefully explained, and resistance should lessen as more employees attend these events and 'spread the word'.

Case-study 2: SCO

SCO, a computer software company founded in the USA, experienced rapid growth during the 1990s. Despite this, SCO found (in line with the general trend) that career opportunities for employees were less frequent and predictable and that their motivation and commitment began to suffer. As a result of a major research project, a plan of action was devised which clearly demonstrated the need to integrate career development with other P&D activities. Macaulay and Harding (1996, 34) list the intentions as being to:

- build a learning culture through greater emphasis on self-development and individual career management
- increase feedback and communications
- raise the effectiveness of the performance management system
- harness the power of employees to bring about change themselves.

To strengthen the emphasis on self-development, career workshops were introduced. Employees were initially concerned that these workshops signified that the employer was abdicating responsibility for their career development. SCO was able to overcome these fears and convey the desired message by a concerted communication effort, using both formal and informal networks. Also, as more people attended and had their misconceptions eradicated, the message was further re-inforced.

Outplacement

Outplacement may be offered to people who are leaving the organisation, voluntarily or otherwise. The term covers a wide range of services, including career counselling and practical help in preparing CVs and identifying job opportunities. All these services are intended to help leavers to prepare for their departure and to plan their future careers and lifestyles.

Outplacement is usually provided by external agencies and may be incorporated into the CAC. There is logic to this approach, because there are common skills and resources needed for career development and outplacement, with obvious economies of scale. The major disadvantage is, as we stated above, that employees might be concerned about the real purpose of the CAC and be reluctant to use its services. A decision has to be made as to whether one centre can be used for these two purposes and, if so, how this difficulty can be overcome.

Case-study 3: Sun, Raychem and Apple

Drawing on the experience of US organisations, Waterman *et al* (1994, 93) highlight the different approaches taken by three companies: Sun, Raychem and Apple. All three have set up CACs as 'havens where employees can go to work on self-assessment, receive counselling, and attend seminars on, say, how to conduct an effective job interview or how to network. They are places where employees can obtain career reference materials, check on internal and external job openings, contribute to discussions on business strategy, and, most important, learn how to think strategically about their own careers.'

There is a difference in their approaches regarding outplacement, however. Raychem decided not to locate outplacement within the CAC so as not to detract from the purposes of both services. Sun and Apple, on the other hand, did incorporate outplacement services into their CACs and took great pains to ensure that, when management encouraged employees to use the CAC, the message was not misinterpreted. They backed this up with a guarantee of confidentiality, such that external agencies were extensively used and managers did not even have the right to know whether their staff had attended.

Career counselling and coaching

Career counselling is a process that enables individuals to recognise and use their resources to manage career-related problems and make career-related decisions. It takes account of the interdependence of career and non-career considerations affecting an individual. Various people may be involved in the process as career counsellors, eg line managers, P&D specialists, assessors at DCs and mentors, as well as external and outplacement consultants. Confidentiality is an obvious concern for people thinking about changing jobs or employers, so organisations may decide to make use of external agencies.

Career coaching is similar to counselling in that it is provided on a one-to-one basis and is client-centred. It also includes directive feedback (ie giving information rather than drawing it out) and training in particular skills.

Career counsellors and coaches need not only to be skilled in these roles but also to be knowledgeable about the options available to an individual. When this is not the case the results are likely to be unsatisfactory to the employee concerned, if not thoroughly demotivating.

Case-study 4: ScottishPower

Regulatory changes have brought about rapid and profound changes in ScottishPower's business in recent times. The IPD Guide (1998, 29) describes how ScottishPower recognised that traditional career paths through the organisation were no longer appropriate and that it needed to encourage employees to consider new career paths incorporating transitions across divisional, functional and geographic boundaries.

To this end, the Power Systems division introduced a programme of career coaching and counselling for managers. The purpose of the programme was to promote individuals' awareness of their own values, to help them see how their

---

career aspirations and objectives were aligned with the organisation's current business and expansion plans, and to prepare them to make the most of opportunities in the organisation as they arose. The programme involved four one-to-one confidential sessions with an external consultant over a two-month period, and included 20 hours' individual work involving self-assessment and practical assignments.

The objectivity of the external consultant has been identified as a key success factor for the programme. Participants valued the fact that the consultants did not necessarily furnish them with answers, or advocate certain courses of action but worked with them through the alternatives in a systematic way in order to find the right *personal* solution.

Mentoring

Mentoring is a well-established career development tool with many advocates. It is based on a relationship between a younger employee and an older, more experienced manager, who is usually not the employee's line manager. The mentor should be familiar with the organisation, its history, politics and culture and be able to provide advice and guidance to the employee on career development. Mentoring may be formal, ie engineered by the organisation, or informal, ie a natural occurrence. There are many benefits to an effective mentoring programme for the individuals concerned, their mentors and the organisation, and such programmes should be linked to other developmental activities such as project work, secondments and work-shadowing.

Like many of the career development interventions listed here, mentoring is a long-term process and, unless properly managed, its outcomes may be unsatisfactory. For instance, mentors and employees may be ill-matched in terms of their personalities, or sufficient time and resources may not have been provided to support the process.

Networking

Most interventions with a career development focus encourage individuals to engage in networking. Arnold (1997, 6) describes it as:

> the effective initiation and maintenance of social relationships for career-related purposes. As careers become less governed by organisational and societal structures, the importance of informal social contacts increases. Furthermore, it is important to have these contacts before one hits times of trouble. They can act as a source of support, advice and information, but one must be prepared to offer these things as well as receive them since, like many social relationships, networking is often based on the social norm of reciprocation. Networking may be particularly important for members of disadvantaged groups who might otherwise find it difficult to gain access to opportunities.

Networking involves the proactive establishment of contacts within and outside the organisation, and it helps to raise the profile of those engaging in it. The benefits to the individual can include finding out about job vacancies that are not formally advertised, gaining support and feedback, and access to a wider range of learning opportunities.

Projects and secondments

Commentators point to a recent trend concerning the emergence of project-based teams for specific business issues. Increasingly, individuals are being required to work on special assignments or projects that take them beyond their normal range of duties. Such work often involves time away from day-to-day activities. Some roles nowadays involve a steady stream of such work. Andrew Mayo (1991, 281) lists the benefits of these experiences:

- the opportunity to gain a deep knowledge of a particular subject
- the opportunity to explore outside the boundaries of the current department – keeping either within organisational boundaries or going beyond them
- the opportunity to enhance a number of personal skills – eg in planning, prioritising, analysing, presenting and communicating
- the opportunity to gain specialised experience of a particular area.

The downside is that, historically, being assigned to work on special projects has been viewed with scepticism and may have reflected badly on outsiders' views of the capabilities of the individuals involved. This is because such work has often been the preserve of individuals approaching retirement whom the organisation wishes to move out of a line management position or because it has been used as a holding post for displaced individuals. This is a pity, because project work can undoubtedly be challenging and stimulating and often proves to be an extremely valuable learning experience.

Associated interventions are secondments, which may be to another division, function, organisation or country. (See Chapter 6 for more information on 'cross-border' workers.) There are many types of secondment, with varying purposes. For instance, graduate trainees often undertake a series of secondments to learn about the business before moving into their chosen specialism. At the other end of the scale, a senior manager might be seconded from the private sector to the public sector (possibly as part of a job exchange) to work on a long-term project.

There are positive spin-offs arising from secondments and, indeed, other interventions that lead to protracted absences from normal duties, including sabbatical leave. They provide opportunities for junior employees to 'act up' in the senior role, although this should involve more than simply 'holding the fort' and trying to avert disasters. Such events need to be carefully planned and managed if they are to be truly developmental experiences for all concerned. However, there is always a downside, and many managers report difficulties in reverting back to their normal duties after a lengthy period of secondment.

Case-study 5: The National Health Service Skill Swap

The internal market in health care has introduced a focus on cost-effectiveness and competition between trusts and health authorities. This, says the IPD Guide (1998, 19), is not a natural climate for investment in staff development, nor for co-operation between competing organisations. The Skill Swap programme has been set up to facilitate collaboration between organisations and to address skill shortages.

The programme enables trusts and health authorities to have short-term consultancy projects conducted by staff seconded from other NHS organisations rather than by expensive external consultants. The programme also enables the individuals who are seconded to broaden their skills and experience by working in other organisations.

The programme originated in the South Thames Region, where the Regional Health Authority (RHA) wanted to look at more imaginative ways of helping District Health Authorities address issues relating to commissioning services from external providers. The RHA reimbursed the home organisation for the cost of replacing the seconded individual. The secondee's services were provided to the host organisation free of charge. Additional consultancy costs, for providing support for secondees, were also met by the RHA. Several other NHS trusts are now exploring how Skill Swap could be used as part of their personal development strategy. A Skill Swap programme has just been completed in the former NHS Women's Unit specifically to develop female middle and senior managers.

Career bridges, lateral moves and development roles

Organisation structures tend to dictate the career ladders that individuals must climb in order to get to the top of their function. There are well-known career ladders for such functions as P&D, sales and marketing, production, design, finance and IT. Technical, professional and academic career ladders usually involve a move into management at some point, eg senior scientists in a laboratory environment and principal lecturers in an educational establishment are the equivalent of middle managers in a financial institution. If the requirements for progress up the hierarchy are known (professional qualifications, specific work experience, the acquisition of certain competencies), such structures tend to work well – until:

- there are insufficient promotion opportunities for capable individuals
- restructuring removes tiers of management, further compounding this problem
- individuals feel trapped in their chosen function and see no way of progressing or changing without having to trade decreased day-to-day involvement in their specialism for greater managerial responsibilities.

In response to these problems, many organisations have introduced career bridges, which facilitate movement across functions and often entail lateral moves to gain new experiences and expertise. Asda Stores are very active in this area and have defined development programmes under the banner of 'So you want to be...', which determine the requirements for progression to specific roles (eg supervisor, department manager and general store manager) as well as career bridges to enable movement across functions, both vertically and laterally.

There are, admittedly, problems with lateral moves:

- Individuals may not view them positively, especially when they are introduced at a time of upheaval or downsizing.
- Managers may resist releasing employees, especially the high-performing ones.
- There may be implications for the reward system – individuals could lose out on performance-related pay, for instance.

To facilitate lateral moves, organisations must seek to promote them as positive and developmental. The culture should be such that departments do not feel that they are in competition with each other but that they are working together for the common good. Finally, employees should not be disadvantaged financially for undertaking a lateral move.

Another initiative promoted by Asda Stores is to specifically identify development roles or positions. The aim is to encourage individuals to broaden their experience either by undertaking additional responsibilities or by adding to their skills portfolio as, say, an internal assessor. Again, the key is to publicise the fact that these are short-term development positions and ensure that the departments concerned are not unduly disrupted by frequent changes of personnel. In choosing such positions you are generally looking for ones where individuals can make a positive contribution quickly without the need for prior specialist knowledge.

> **Case-study 6: Philips Research Laboratories (PRL)**
>
> Philips Research Laboratories is staffed by highly qualified scientists engaged in a range of research activities. The organisation makes use of a number of career development interventions, including development roles and a dual-career ladder structure. The dual-career ladder, for technical and managerial progression, provides employees with an opportunity to rise to a very senior level on the basis of technical capability, as opposed to moving into a more generalist managerial role, and is designed to achieve two things of significance in a highly technical environment. Firstly, it avoids the possibility of making outstanding technical people into

mediocre managers in order to promote them, and secondly it demonstrates publicly the extent to which the organisation values outstanding technical ability. See the chart below.

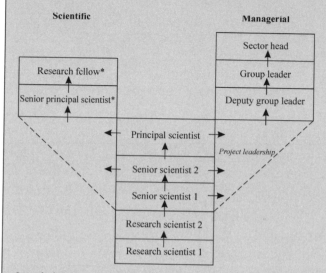

Scientific　　　　　　　　　　　**Managerial**

* may also have project leadership responsibilities

At the same time, those who demonstrate the appropriate skills and interests may be given project leadership responsibilities as a means of testing and developing their managerial potential. In announcing the recent creation of research fellow, as an additional level at the top of the technical ladder, Managing Director Peter Saraga said:

> I believe the creation of research fellow positions within our organisation will both enhance our technical career structure by giving recognition to our most outstanding scientists and provide the strategic technical influence on the direction of our research programmes essential to maintaining PRL's place in the top league of industrial electronics research laboratories.

Case-study and chart reproduced with the kind permission of Philips Research Laboratories

Educational sponsorship and accredited training

Organisations have for many years provided financial support to employees studying for educational and professional qualifications. Yet, all too often, little thought is given to this process, and sponsorship is granted on a first-come first-served basis and depends on the perceived relevance of the desired qualification. Also, individuals may find that they are suddenly denied further funding midway through a programme of study because of newly imposed budget constraints. A planned and integrated programme of career development would enable a clearer setting of priorities and a longer-term focus that would avoid the 'You've had your turn, so now go to the back of the queue' approach.

Training is, obviously, necessary to assist employees in acquiring the skills and knowledge to perform their current duties as well as in realising their potential. Often, however, it is viewed as an input, and there is only a limited attempt to recognise and value the outcome, ie the learning that has taken place. Further, when applying for positions outside the organisation individuals may find that there is little significance attached to their training records.

Employers should therefore seek to ensure that, wherever possible, the training that they provide is accredited by a relevant body, eg the IPD or City and Guilds, so that it is nationally recognised (in the spirit of such initiatives as NVQs). Asda Stores are again leaders in this area: they have an 'academy scheme' that seeks to recognise the acquisition of such craft skills as meat, bakery, green grocery and wines and spirits. In line with many Asda training programmes, all such training is accredited by the relevant professional body. Fears that such moves may increase employees' marketability and lead to higher turnover have to be balanced by the fact that visible career development is a huge aid to recruitment and retention. The Asda Academy of Craft Skills has been so successful that it reached the finals for two National Training Awards in 1999.

Future initiatives

In brief, these are likely to include:

- increased use of IT to allow more open communication about career development opportunities within other divisions, functions and associated organisations, and across national boundaries
- increased use of person-posting (as opposed to job-posting), where individuals self-advertise their availability and aspirations on the internal network
- establishing commercial CACs for groups of subscribing organisations. Such a move provides excellent networking opportunities and allows for creative interorganisational career development strategies.

End-note

1 Reprinted by permission of Paul Chapman Publishing Ltd from J. Arnold, *Managing Careers into the 21st Century,* © J. Arnold 1997.

How do we make career development work?

A partnership approach

Many people report that it is only when they are under threat of redundancy and eligible for outplacement services that they come to realise they have transferable skills. The reason may be because this is the first time they have carried out any form of self-assessment to identify their skills, strengths and attributes. Such knowledge is obviously

55

useful to the individual concerned but will be lost to the employing organisation if it is discovered only at the point of termination.

There are therefore several advantages to a partnership approach, organisations and individuals taking equal responsibility for career development. They include:

- the greater knowledge that organisations are able to gain about what individuals can offer in their current jobs and in future roles. The accumulation of this information is equivalent to a 'skills bank' which the organisation can draw on and add to by developing other skills considered crucial for future success.

- the ability to reconcile the different perspectives of individuals and organisations regarding career development. These two perspectives must be recognised and openly discussed, and attempts must be made to seek mutually acceptable solutions. Further, individuals' perspectives should be regularly reviewed to see whether any changes have occurred, eg in circumstances and career aspirations.

- the ability to minimise the impact of anti-career drivers, such as rationalisation programmes, and promote pro-development drivers, such as self-managed careers. Without a continuous dialogue between managers and employees, these forces will pull in opposite directions and the two parties will not be encouraged to look at alternative ways to develop careers.

A framework for design and implementation

If you are considering introducing a new career development programme into your organisation or are revising the existing one, you would be wise to adopt a structured approach. A framework is suggested below. You should note that these 10 steps are not discrete ones – for example, publicity is an ongoing process, and choosing consultants may need to be tackled earlier or later than suggested, depending on the consultants' role. The steps are:

1. auditing the current situation
2. establishing the key issues
3. reviewing the options
4. integrating with other P&D activities
5. choosing consultants
6. agreeing an action plan
7. setting up the support mechanisms
8. piloting
9. publicising and implementing
10. evaluating success.

A useful starting-point is the establishment of a working party, drawn from all sectors of the workforce and led by a senior board member, who will be seen as the champion of any resultant proposals for career development. The working party needs to agree its terms of reference and ought to contain representatives from management, trade unions (if applicable), P&D and employees drawn from the various levels and functions within the organisation and representative of the profile of the workforce (based on race, gender, age, disability etc). The working party has varying roles to play in all of the following stages.

Auditing the current situation

This involves taking a broad view of the organisational and individual perspectives on career development to establish a starting-point. The current career development provisions should be reviewed to establish whether they are working satisfactorily. This information can be gained from a number of sources, including company documentation, such as statistical information, reports and notes of meetings, and from discussions with managers at all levels, P&D specialists, employee representatives and other employees. In order to gain comprehensive information, you may decide to undertake an attitude survey, because this would help to identify the key concerns of the majority of your staff.

The IPD Guide (1998, 11–12) suggests that, in undertaking this audit, you should seek answers to such questions as these:

- *From the individual perspective*, what does it mean to have a career in this organisation? How central is the organisation to individuals' careers? Do they see it as a stepping-stone or as a job for life? What do people think of the formal and informal career management systems or processes that are in place?
- *From the organisational perspective*, what is the real purpose of career and skill development in the organisation? Is it to develop skills to meet immediate business needs? Is it to develop future business leaders? Is it to keep employees motivated and to retain them? What challenges is the business facing that are people-related?

You will also need to establish whether your existing career development interventions are vertically integrated with the business goals and horizontally integrated with other P&D activities, and whether the latter are integrated with each other (see below).

Establishing the key issues

The results of your research should enable you to draw some conclusions about the key issues. For example, one of your major concerns may be that you have an ageing workforce but no clear succession plans in place to fill future vacancies for senior managers. We noted in Chapter 5 that there were five main purposes for career development: assessment, career options, action-planning, skill development and vacancy-filling. Here your purposes are centred on skill development and vacancy-filling. Alternatively, you may be expecting a dramatic reduction in the workforce across all levels over the next 12 months. Your purposes would then be to encourage assessment and discuss career options. Finally, individuals may feel that self-management is not working, because they are not getting enough company support. Your purpose here may be to implement more formal career development interventions to aid action-planning as a joint activity. (The graphic on page 36 provides information on which types of intervention are pertinent to the five main purposes, although most can be used for more than one purpose.)

Reviewing the options

The working party should now review the various career development interventions available to it, consulting as large a section of the workforce as possible. (See Chapter 5 for examples and an exploration of their pros and cons.)

The choice of interventions depends primarily on the purposes of career development within the organisation. A manageable number of suitable interventions should be chosen in the first instance, on the premise that others can always be added at a later stage. In deciding on this choice, a number of other important factors should be considered:

- the *organisational culture*, because dramatic changes in approach (eg from centralised succession-planning to job-posting and the establishment of peer centres) will not be readily accepted by employees who have not previously been encouraged to undertake self-assessment and proactively promote their career plans; the culture needs to be an open and supportive one that will not stifle change
- the *timing of the intervention*, eg the introduction of DCs should not coincide with a major redundancy programme
- the *size of the organisation*, because smaller enterprises do not require, or are unable to sustain, the same range of interventions as larger ones (see Chapter 7 for more information on this)
- the *financial resources available*, because some alternatives such as CACs and DCs are considerably more expensive to implement and maintain than others
- the *availability of expertise* within the organisation to resource the interventions
- the *difficulties in releasing individuals* from their jobs; organisations should seek to provide a mix of opportunities, some involving time away from the

workplace, but others, such as on-the-job coaching, incurring only minor disruption to day-to-day activities.

Integration with other P&D activities

Before making a final choice of career development interventions, you should check whether they will 'fit' with other P&D activities. You will be seeking to establish the following: What are the links, and do they coincide or conflict? What information exchanges are necessary between these processes? Are any of your initial choices ruled out because of potential conflicts? Conversely, can existing P&D activities be changed to accommodate your best choices?

Two examples demonstrate this last point:

- Imagine a scenario in which vacancies at senior levels are not openly advertised but selected personnel are either appointed outright or are invited to apply. Such a closed and secretive practice is likely to be contrary to interventions that encourage a proactive self-management approach. An integrated career development process would result in the halting of the above practice and the open advertising of *all* vacancies.
- In this scenario, the company in question currently recognises increased status and responsibility (ie progression through the ranks) with enhanced financial packages. New career development interventions such as lateral moves and development roles would not attract any increased financial rewards under the existing system. An integrated career development process

would result in a revision of the whole reward structure to accommodate recognition of increased flexibility and the acquisition of new skills (eg competency-based pay).

Choosing consultants

You may decide that the additional work created by the introduction or revision of a career development pro-gramme can be absorbed internally, and there are obvious benefits attached to line-management involvement in developing the careers of their staff. You should, however, consider where help from outside agencies would be bene-ficial, especially where there is limited expertise internally or confidentiality is an important issue This may be in any or all of the following stages: auditing, design, the provision of specialist services and evaluation.

In any event, you should follow the steps below to ensure that the ensuing relationship is a successful one:

- Clearly define the project, eg objectives, boundaries, performance standards, logistics, time-scales and resources.
- Invite tenders and select an initial short-list.
- Provide a comprehensive briefing to those short-listed.
- Arrange for those short-listed to make presenta-tions, including detailed, costed proposals.
- Assess the proposals against your project objectives and consider such factors as credibility, depth of knowledge and expertise, track records and the availability of support services (rather than cost alone).

- Take up references before making a final selection.

NB: This stage may need to be tackled earlier or later, depending on the consultants' role or roles.

Agreeing an action plan

Having selected a number of suitable interventions, a detailed action plan should now be drafted. This must cover the:

- proposed interventions
- practical outcomes sought
- priorities within the list of actions
- detailed stages for implementation and who is responsible
- support systems necessary, eg training, reward and use of external agencies
- mechanisms for evaluating success
- cost of these proposals and the benefits of implementation in terms of business objectives, saved costs, increased revenue etc.

The working party should consult on the details of these proposals as widely as possible before presenting to the board a final draft for approval. Included in these consultations should be the managers who will be implementing the programme.

Setting up the support mechanisms

On the assumption that you will be making use of some externally provided support services, you will need to finalise the arrangements to ensure that these are firmly in place before the pilot and fully operational for the launch.

Logistical issues such as office space are amongst the details that require careful consideration.

Career development interventions necessitate line managers' fulfilling a number of support roles – as mentors, coaches and assessors. Line managers will undoubtedly bear the brunt of the responsibility, especially for the less formal activities, and must therefore have time and resources at their disposal in order to fulfil their obligations to their staff. P&D specialists have facilitative roles to play here. This includes ensuring that developmental initiatives such as job exchanges, placements and cover for sabbatical leave take place and are not hampered by bureaucratic inertia.

As well as requiring initial training to familiarise themselves with the new programme, line managers may also require additional training to ensure that they possess the requisite knowledge, eg of career development opportunities across (and possibly beyond) the organisation, and the skills needed to ensure effective appraisal interviewing, informal counselling and constructive feedback.

Employees must be made aware of these services and the procedures for making use of them, as well as any 'rules' regarding time spent away from the workplace. P&D specialists are likely to provide the initial point of contact for employee enquiries and may be charged with monitoring and maintaining the programme.

Piloting

Rather than launch the full career development programme with a big fanfare, it is sensible to start with a small pilot scheme. This avoids expensive and time-consuming errors and allows alternative approaches to be tried out. You need to choose a discrete section of the organisation for the pilot, but one that is reasonably representative of the whole. Implement the chosen interventions for a realistic but limited period of time. Next, gather feedback on the pilot scheme from all participants and make changes to the overall action plan where necessary.

Publicising and implementing

How should you publicise your new programme? There are several options, and you should plan to undertake some or all of the following:

- Announce the new initiative and its purpose (or purposes) with a letter from the managing director or chief executive.
- Introduce the new programme by carrying out a series of briefings for line managers, other key personnel and union/employee representatives.
- Issue a manual to managers indicating the procedures to be followed and factual information such as contacts, resources etc.
- Provide written information for all employees, eg in an explanatory booklet, describing what employees can expect from the organisation and what part they are expected to play.
- Re-inforce the message via existing communication mechanisms such as team briefings and internal newsletters.
- Change relevant procedures, eg the applications procedure for educational sponsorship, and revise the staff handbook to reflect the new programme.
- Insert an appropriate sentence into

advertisements for job vacancies (internal and external).

● Include references to the programme in job interviews and at induction.

● Continue the process by announcing 'successes', eg staff movements and achievements.

Finally, with regard to implementation, put into effect the final action plan, taking account of the priorities, costings, time-scales and responsibilities.

Evaluating success

Career development is, by its nature, a long-term process, so interventions must be allowed sufficient time to 'bed in' before evaluation. It may take several years before you can fully assess whether your career development interventions have been successful. There are, however, a number of monitoring mechanisms that may be useful to you in the shorter term, eg:

● the number of people leaving through career frustration

● the difficulties experienced in filling vacancies

● the breadth of functional or specialist experience in top teams

● improved individual performances, measured through the appraisal scheme

● the achievement of performance objectives and targets

● the number of eg project-based assignments, secondments, exchanges of staff and career changes (within the organisation)

- the number of people making use of CAC facilities
- the number of people attending DCs, and their subsequent progress
- the feelings of employees about their career development and knowledge of available opportunities, indicated through appraisals and attitude surveys
- the continuing visibility of the career development programme, eg statements from the chief executive, publicity information, inclusion in team briefings
- the accuracy of the knowledge base regarding workers' skills, abilities and aspirations
- the range of career development interventions available
- comparison of these activities with those of benchmark organisations
- the results of specific evaluation processes on, say, training, coaching and counselling activities
- the outcomes of outplacement services, eg the percentage of successful placements.

These measures help to determine the effectiveness of the programme, but periodically a major review will be necessary to ensure that career development is achieving its purposes and continues to be integrated both vertically and horizontally within the organisation. The results need then to be fed back in so that the career development programme evolves to reflect the changing needs of the organisation and the individuals within it.

Pitfalls

Because you are dealing with a programme of change, you will inevitably encounter some pitfalls along the way. Examples of these, and the means to overcome them, are highlighted below:

Lack of visible support from the top

The champions of career development must be proactive in persuading senior managers of its importance. Board members need then to show a visible commitment by talking to employees and being involved in publicity materials, and by attending relevant events, eg career workshops and the opening ceremony for a CAC.

Unsupportive organisational culture

Such a culture may lead employees to be sceptical about the career development programme and be unwilling to get involved. This may be because they have recently survived a major redundancy exercise and their confidence has not been restored, or simply because they are suffering from 'initiative overload'. Organisations must first tackle these issues and then take a step-by-step approach to introducing career development, following the guidance above.

Inconsistent application of career development

Interventions may work well in some areas of the business but not in others. Andrew Mayo (1991, 305) spells out the series of conflicts faced by line managers that can lead to these inconsistencies:

- the wish, even the need, to retain the best people rather than lose them to career progression elsewhere

- the stronger pull of the expedient short-term decision against the longer-term pay-off of more strategic choices
- the choice of an already experienced candidate for a job against a person who needs it for his or her personal development
- the pressures of each day as against the need to spend time in coaching people or updating them on career breaks
- the easy choice of training courses for personal growth rather than the discipline of defining a learning need and choosing the best option
- the desire to decentralise accountability and the need to co-ordinate the development of capability for the good of the organisation as a whole.

These conflicts must be recognised and, where managers' actions do not fall into line with the organisation's philosophy on career development, their decisions must be challenged. Again we can see the need for an organisational culture that promotes and supports career development if it is to have any chance of success.

A recipe for success

We have throughout this chapter attempted to emphasise good practice in delivering career development. Hirsh and Jackson (1996, 25) point to research indicating that the recipe for success in career development terms is:

- an appropriate and honest message – clarifying what organisations really want over time from their employees

- workable career development processes – based on a clear view of the needs of individuals and their managers
- a real intention to deliver – fewer interventions, properly supported and sustained, are likely to be much more effective.

How do we motivate special groups of workers?

Equality of opportunity

We have stressed throughout this book the need to provide equality of opportunity in career development for all employees. Legislation in this area makes specific provisions regarding the need to protect workers from discrimination on the grounds of race, gender or disability. Good practice also dictates that organisations should extend this to ensure non-discriminatory treatment on the grounds of age, hours of work, sexual orientation etc. In other words, all career development decisions should be based on objective criteria only.

That said, some groups of workers may need special attention because they have in the past been disadvantaged by (or even ignored by) career development programmes. We shall deal with a number of these groups below.

Women

It is well documented that few women actually make it to the top of organisations: there is a glass ceiling limiting their career progression. Commentators have differing views on why this is. Career breaks, differences in management or leadership styles between women and men, a lack of confidence or self-belief in women, the burden of childcare and domestic responsibilities, and prejudice on the part of male managers feature among the more popular views. There is statistical evidence to show that the underrepresentation of women in management is not explained by their educational qualifications, which compare well with those of men. Women do, however, sometimes:

- choose jobs with poor career prospects, eg secretarial and clerical work
- follow different functional careers from men's within organisations, ie they are more likely to be located in support functions such as administration and personnel than in line-management positions
- stay longer as specialists within one function, whereas men move more quickly into generalist roles
- make slower early career progress than their male counterparts, even when they have been recruited on a 'fast-track' basis.

Whatever the causes – the choices made by women them-selves or the results of stereotyping and discrimination – women now make up nearly 50 per cent of the workforce, so organisations cannot afford to ignore their career development needs. Traditional career development frameworks, with their concentration on organisational prerogatives and a reluctance to take account of individuals' needs and family circumstances, have favoured male career progress and done little to help and encourage women, especially those with family responsibilities. Even family-friendly policies, which have helped some women to remain in or return to the workplace – such policies as career breaks, part-time work, job-sharing and homework-ing - have actually compounded the problem, because these women have come to be viewed as having no interest in their career progression.

To resolve these difficulties, organisations must:

- ensure that equal access to opportunities for training, development and promotion is available to all, and that women are not disadvantaged, regardless of their working arrangements
- make special arrangements, where women are underrepresented in senior positions, to encourage women to take responsibility for their own career development by engaging in self-development, career-planning, networking etc. (See Case-study 1 on page 39 for an example of this.)

Ethnic minorities

The situation for members of ethnic minority groups is very similar to that of women. Statistics show that ethnic minorities in the UK suffer higher levels of unemployment and are underrepresented at all levels of organisations, particularly in managerial positions.

It makes sense for organisations to capitalise on the talent of all their workers (and potential workers), so the actions that should be taken are similar to those listed above:

- Organisations should ensure that all their decisions regarding career development are objective and based on merit.
- Where ethnic minorities are underrepresented, positive action should be taken and the individuals concerned encouraged to adopt self-development and self-assessment processes.

Plateaued managers

The pyramidal structure of most organisations means that many managers will inevitably reach a stage where they (and others) perceive that they have climbed to the highest level of responsibility they are likely to achieve. Recent developments such as shortened hierarchies and decentralised operations have meant that more, and younger, employees will arrive at career plateaux rather earlier than expected and regardless of their performance.

It is worth pointing out that the above statement relies on the traditional definition of a career, ie one defined by upward and promotional advances only. Nevertheless, what is needed is a change in attitudes and culture so that career bridges, lateral moves, project work, development roles and secondments are all viewed in a positive light as helpful to long-term career development. Career-plateauing could become a thing of the past if the reduction in opportunities for promotion is balanced by unlimited opportunities for development.

In any event, as we have already stated, line managers have an extremely important role to play in the career development programme. This in itself should prove to be a developmental experience for them and will lead to the acquisition or further development of specific skills, such as mentoring, coaching, assessing and giving feedback. Involvement of line managers in the more formal aspects of your career development programme, such as CACs and DCs, could also open up lines of communication across functions and levels of the hierarchy which will improve your 'visibility' and facilitate networking. This will be especially beneficial in the case of older managers, because it will confirm to them that their experience and skills are still highly valued by the organisation.

Flexible workers

As we stated in Chapter 2, there is a trend among organisations to operate with a much more flexible workforce than in the past. There is less reliance on full-time 'permanent' contracts of employment and greater use of:

- part-time contracts and job-sharing arrangements
- temporary posts
- fixed-term contracts

- casual and agency staff
- externally-based consultants and associates.

This has implications for organisations. Clearly, they wish to invest in the training and development necessary to equip these flexible workers to do their contracted jobs satisfactorily; a longer-term view, however, would take account of the fact that these flexible workers may have a long-term relationship with the organisation. Organisations should therefore consider investing in updating their knowledge and skills, particularly where these requirements are rapidly changing or are likely to be in short supply in the future. Further, some organisations, such as commercial training and educational providers, operate with a tiny core of key employees and rely heavily on their peripheral workforce of associates. Let's be very clear about it: there are pitfalls ahead for employers who fail to develop their workers. To cite a few examples:

- Failure to ensure that associates have up-to-date skills and knowledge may result in poor customer service and loss of future business.
- Failure to make full use of the potential of these workers, eg by tapping into unused organisational and managerial skills, may lead to frustration on the part of associates and decisions to search for alternative work.
- Failure to encourage a mutual interest in career development will do little to invoke loyalty and commitment from these workers.

Employees in SMEs

Recent figures show that there is a significant growth in the number of firms employing fewer than 20 people and that such small and medium-sized enterprises (SMEs) account in general for a large proportion of total employment. We should therefore not be concentrating just on large organisations when considering career development interventions.

What effect does the size of an organisation have on career development? To answer this, we must first make some generalised comparisons between smaller and larger organisations. Smaller organisations tend to:

- have informal organisation structures with fewer hierarchical levels and, potentially, better communications
- have fewer formal planning processes, so approaches to training and development and succession-planning may be more *ad hoc*
- require greater flexibility and a greater range of skills from their staff
- experience a higher rate of labour turnover.

It may, therefore, be more difficult to institute formal processes for career development within smaller organisations. However, there are many advantages in career development terms for employees working in SMEs. As the IPD Guide (1998, 32) puts it:

> Employees often have exposure to a wide selection of business activities, develop a broad range of skills, and are flexible in the range of tasks they accomplish. The informal structure of a small

company – even one that is relatively mature – may mean that employees have more opportunity to be creative about how they go about their work. A company that is growing rapidly offers the individuals within it a range of opportunities for developing their roles, setting up new projects and taking on extra responsibilities.

In summary, employees in SMEs may need to consider moving to another organisation if they are seeking career progression in the traditional sense, but others may decide to trade frequent promotion for higher levels of responsibility and autonomy than would be available in a more specialised position in a larger organisation. Both sets of individuals may still justifiably consider themselves to have successful careers.

Cross-border workers

International assignments have long been recognised as excellent learning opportunities for individuals. From the organisational perspective, they are also an important element of staff development and succession-planning, as well as a means of transferring skills and knowledge between operations in different countries.

In the past, employees working for multinational corporations realised that refusal of an overseas assignment would be likely to have a detrimental effect on their careers. Nowadays, employers need to recognise that, as with all career development interventions, the management of overseas assignments has to take account of individual and organisational perspectives. There are two main courses of action:

- Organisations must tailor assignments to individuals' needs. This may involve compromises on the duration and timing of the assignment, additional finances where partners and families are affected, and guarantees, wherever possible, regarding future roles on return to the UK.
- Where individuals do decline such opportunities, it should be made clear to all concerned that this will not limit future opportunities either in the UK or abroad.

See Appendix 2 regarding the relevant legislation in this area.

What are the key points?

1   The changing context within which organisations operate has resulted in the demise of the traditional upwardly mobile career. Careers should now be viewed in a wider sense as applying to all workers and encompassing a range of occupational experiences, not just conventional ones.

2   Career development should be available to all staff and should not concentrate on just the élite few. There is a need to balance organisational and individual perspectives in career development. Without it, organisations will fail to capitalise on the talents and potential of their staff.

3   There is no specific legislative right to career development but there are associated employment rights relating to contracts, training and discrimination. Some of these rights are being extended beyond 'employees' to cover 'workers'.

4   People develop through a combination of training and experience, the latter being by far the more important. The responsibility for career

development should be a shared one between employer and employee, ie a partnership approach.

5   Promotion opportunities are nowadays even more limited than in the past but there are unlimited opportunities for personal and, therefore, career development.

6   There is a wide range of career development interventions to choose from. Your choice will depend on a number of factors, including the purposes, the organisational culture and size, timing, the availability of resources and the career goals and objectives of your staff.

7   For the best chance of success, you should select a limited number of well-resourced interventions.

8   There are many pitfalls to be aware of when implementing a programme of change. Career development interventions need to be fully integrated with your business goals and other P&D activities and they require visible support from top management, a supportive organisational culture and consistent application.

9   Special attention may need to be paid to certain groups of workers, including women, ethnic minorities, plateaued managers, flexible workers, employees in SMEs and cross-border workers.

10 You should adopt a step-by-step approach to the design and implementation of your career development programme, ensuring that you undertake an initial audit, consult as widely as possible, carry out a pilot scheme and make provisions for ongoing evaluation.

Appendix 1:
Employment statistics

Jackson *et al* (1996, 15–21), the Office for National Statistics, and the Labour Force Survey provide some useful statistics and predictions on the following:

- demographic and labour market trends
- education and qualifications
- changing patterns of employment
- unemployment.

Demographic and labour market trends

- By 2001 34 per cent of the labour force will be over 45 years old, and this percentage is forecast to go on increasing.
- By 2006 women will make up 46 per cent of the UK labour force and have an economic activity rate of 75 per cent (although many will continue to be in part-time employment).

Education and qualifications

- The proportion of the UK population obtaining at least some educational qualifications rose from about one third to two thirds between 1971 and 1992.
- The number of first-degree graduates rose by 65 per cent between 1981 and 1997.

Changing patterns of employment

- In 1994 women made up 83 per cent of all part-time workers; 46 per cent of women in employment worked part-time.
- Firms employing fewer than 20 people created a million additional jobs between 1985 and 1989 and a further 350,000 jobs between 1989 and 1991. This trend has continued to rise throughout the 1990s.
- In 1998 there were 3.3 million self-employed people (over 14 per cent of the employed population). This growth in self-employment has taken place at a faster rate than in any other EU country (and is also growing faster among women than men).
- Between 1991 and 2000 there will be an additional 1.7 million managerial, professional and technical jobs but the numbers employed in manual, clerical and secretarial work will continue to decline.

Unemployment

- Unemployment reached a peak of 2.9 million in 1993 and has steadily fallen since then to about 1.8 million in 1998.
- Unemployment rates are higher among men, ethnic minorities, the disabled and the young, although the majority of long-term unemployed people are in the higher age brackets. There are also regional and subregional variations.

These statistics © Institute for Employment Studies 1996

(see Jackson 1996)

Appendix 2:
The legal issues

There is no legal entitlement to career development, but it is worth pointing out a number of related legislative provisions, mostly in the fields of contracts, training and discrimination. They are summarised below.

Contracts of employment

Many career development interventions, particularly those requiring a change of duties and possibly location, will by their nature result in a change to the terms and conditions of employment. In the absence of flexibility clauses allowing such changes, employers should consult the employees concerned and seek their acceptance of the proposed changes, rather than impose them unilaterally. If they follow the latter course, they may find themselves facing constructive dismissal claims.

Access to training and promotion

The Sex Discrimination Act 1975, the Race Relations Act 1976 and the Disability Discrimination Act 1995 make it unlawful for employers to discriminate on the grounds of gender, race or disability 'in the way in which they afford access to opportunities for promotion, transfer or training'. There is also a requirement under the Companies/Directors' Report (Employment of Disabled Persons) Regulations 1980 that directors' reports must contain a note regarding the policy that the organisation has applied for 'the training, career development and promotion of the disabled employed by the company'.

Ageism

Unlike in the USA, it is not yet illegal in the UK to discriminate against people on the grounds of age, although the Labour government has issued a code of practice to discourage this widespread practice. Like all discrimination, ageism is potentially wasteful of valuable resources.

Study leave

The Right to Time Off for Study or Training Regulations 1999 provide an entitlement to reasonable paid time off for study or training for eligible young employees.

Part-time workers

The Part-Time Workers Directive, which is expected to be implemented in the UK during 2000, aims to remove discrimination against part-time workers and to improve the quality of part-time work. The Directive requires employers to ensure that part-time workers have the same rights as full-time workers in respect of key benefits, including opportunities for training and promotion.

Posted workers

These are workers posted to another country within the EU. The Posted Workers Directive, implemented in the UK in September 1999, provides posted workers with the same minimal levels of protection and employment as those applying to UK-based employees. Thus the anti-discrimination rights listed under 'Access to training and promotion' above now also specifically apply to this group of workers.

Workers' rights

The rights relating to unfair dismissal, redundancy pay, maternity and statutory time off are currently only available to employees. It is worth noting, however, that the anti-discrimination Acts go further, and individuals working under contracts of service, rather than contracts of employment, may in certain circumstances be protected against sex, race or disability discrimination, which is, by definition, illegal.

Further, we have witnessed in the UK a trend of new employment rights being extended from 'employees' to 'workers', which can cover anyone but the genuinely self-employed.

Rights to information

The Data Protection Act 1998 extends the rights of employees to obtain access to data that concerns them. A particular right of interest here concerns the processing of personal data by automatic means. Where that automatic processing is the sole means of making a decision that will significantly affect the data subject, the individual is entitled to be informed 'of the logic involved in that decision-making'. This has implications for succession-planning and career development, but there is an exemption whereby individuals are not entitled to information in circumstances where personal data are to be processed for the purpose of 'management forecasting or management planning'. Before you breathe a sigh of relief, please note that the exemption applies only insofar as the provision of the information 'would be likely to prejudice the conduct of that business or other activity'. Case-law should help to determine how widely this exemption is construed in practice. In the meantime, due care should be exercised when handling data pertaining to succession-planning and career development.

Consultation rights

The Employment Relations Act 1999 makes some changes to the collective consultation rights in the workplace. Specifically, with regard to training, trade unions are entitled to be consulted about the employer's policy on and plans for training regarding those workers within the bargaining unit.

References and bibliography

ARNOLD J. (1997) *Managing Careers into the 21st Century.* London, Paul Chapman Publishing.

GUEST D. (1995) 'Why do people work?' Presentation to the Institute of Personnel and Development National Conference, Harrogate, October.

GUEST D. *and* MACKENZIE DAVEY K. (1996) 'Don't write off the traditional career'. *People Management.* 22 February. pp22–5.

HIRSH W. *and* JACKSON C. (1996) 'Ticket to ride or no place to go?' *People Management.* 27 June. pp20–23, 25.

HOLBECHE L. (1995) 'Peering into the future of careers'. *People Management.* 31 May. pp26–8.

HOLBECHE L. (1996) 'Developing people in changing structures'. *Training Officer.* Vol.32, No.5, June. pp146–8.

IPD GUIDE (1998) *Career Management in Organisations.* London, Institute of Personnel and Development.

JACKSON C. *and* HIRSH W. (1991) 'Women managers and career progression: the British experience'. *Women in Management Review and Abstracts.* Vol.6, No.2. pp10–16.

JACKSON C. (1996) 'Managing careers in 2000 and beyond'. *Training Officer.* Vol.32, No.9. November. pp262–4.

JACKSON C., ARNOLD J., NICHOLSON N. *and* WATTS A.G. (1996) *Managing Careers in 2000 and beyond.* Sussex, Institute for Employment Studies.

JAMES P. *and* WARK V. (1995) 'Replacing the ladders'. *People Management.* 31 May. pp28–9, 31.

MACAULAY S. *and* HARDING N. (1996) 'Drawing up a new careers contract'. *People Management.* 4 April. pp34–5.

MARSHALL J. (1995) *Women Managers Moving on.* London, Routledge.

MAYO A. (1991) *Managing Careers: Strategies for organisations.* London, Institute of Personnel Management.

MAYO A. (1992) 'A framework for career management'. *Personnel Management.* February. pp36–9.

MUMFORD A. (1998) *Developing Top Managers.* Aldershot, Gower.

NATHAN R. *and* HILL L. (1992) *Career Counselling.* London, Sage.

PEDLER M., BURGOYNE J. *and* BOYDELL T. (1986) *A Manager's Guide to Self-Development.* Maidenhead, McGraw-Hill.

PEMBERTON C. (1998) *Strike a New Career Deal: Build a great future in the changing world of work.* London, Pitman Publishing.

PEMBERTON C., REFAUSSE J. *and* EVANS C. (1998) *Managing Career Dilemmas in the New World of Work.* London, Financial Times Management. Pearson Education Ltd.

REYNOLDS A., SAMBROOK S. *and* STEWART J. (1997) *Dictionary of HRD.* Aldershot. Gower.

TRACEY W. R. (1991) *The Human Resources Glossary.* New York, Amacom.

WATERMAN R. H. Jr, WATERMAN J. A. *and* COLLARD B. A. (1994) 'Towards a career-resilient workforce'. *Harvard Business Review.* July-August. pp87–95.

WHIDDETT S. *and* HOLLYFORDE S. (1999) *The Competencies Handbook*. London, Institute of Personnel and Development.

IPD Publications

With some 100,000 members, the **Institute of Personnel and Development** is the largest organisation in Europe dealing with the management and development of people. The IPD operates its own publishing unit, producing books and research reports for human resource practitioners, students, and general managers charged with people management responsibilities.

Currently there are over 150 titles, covering the full range of personnel and development issues. The books have been commissioned from leading experts in the field and are packed with the latest information and guidance to best practice.

For free copies of the IPD Books Catalogue, please contact the publishing department:

Tel.: 020-8263 3387
Fax: 020-8263 3850
E-mail: publish@ipd.co.uk
Web: http://www.ipd.co.uk/publications

Orders for books should be sent direct to:

Plymbridge Distributors
Estover
Plymouth
Devon
PL6 7PZ

Credit card orders:
Tel.: 01752 202 301
Fax: 01752 202 333

INSTITUTE OF PERSONNEL
AND DEVELOPMENT

Customer Satisfaction Survey

We would be grateful if you could spend a few minutes answering these questions and return the postcard to IPD. <u>Please use a black pen to answer</u>. If you would like to receive a free IPD pen, please include your name and address.

....

1. Title of book ....

2. Date of purchase: month .... year ....

3. How did you buy this book?
   ☐ Bookshop ☐ Mail order ☐ Exhibition

4. If ordered by mail, how long did it take to arrive:
   ☐ 1 week ☐ 2 weeks ☐ more than 2 weeks

5. Name of shop .... Town.. Country ....

6. Please grade the following according to their influence on your purchasing decision with 1 as least influential: (please tick)

	1	2	3	4	5
Title					
Publisher					
Author					
Price					
Subject					

7. On a scale of 1 to 5 (with 1 as poor & 5 as excellent) please give your impressions of the book in terms of: (please tick)

	1	2	3	4	5
Cover design					
Page design					
Paper/print quality					
Good value for money					

8. Did you find the book:
   Covers the subject in sufficient depth ☐ Yes ☐ No
   Useful for your work ☐ Yes ☐ No

9. Are you using this book to help:
   ☐ In your work ☐ Personal study ☐ Both ☐ Other (please state) ....

Please complete if you are using this as part of a course

10. Name of academic institution...

11. Name of course you are following? ....

12. Did you find this book relevant to the syllabus? ☐ Yes ☐ No ☐ Don't know

Thank you!

To receive regular information about IPD books and resources call 0181 263 3387.
Any data or information provided to the IPD for the purposes of membership and other Institute activities will be processed by means of a computer database or otherwise. You may, from time to time, receive business information relevant to your work from the Institute and its other activities. If you do not wish to receive such information please write to the IPD, giving your full name, address and postcode. The Institute does not make its membership lists available to any outside organisation.

BUSINESS REPLY SERVICE
Licence No WD 1019

Publishing Department

Institute of Personnel and Development

IPD House

Camp Road

Wimbledon

London

SW19 4BR